GERMAN

LEARN 35 WORDS TO SPEAK GERMAN

Written by Peter and Helena Roberts

For the first-time visitor to Germany or Austria

An English/German language book, teaching you how to speak German using 35 selected useful words.

First edition: September 2017
v1.0 : Sept. 2017

Published in the United Kingdom
by
Russet Publishing
russetpublishing.com

Distributed internationally
by
Lulu Press Inc.
Raleigh, North Carolina, USA
lulu.com

Printed version
ISBN 978-1-910537-25-1

Not available as an electronic version

Copyright © 2017 Peter and Helena Roberts

Comments and corrections welcome to
peter.roberts@russetpublishing.com

"Learn 35 Words to Speak" is the copyright trade phrase
of Peter and Helena Roberts.

A WORD FROM THE AUTHORS

The German in this book was written by a competent German speaker, but the work has been further translated, proof read, and certified by a qualified German national—see the bottom of this page.

This book has been made for absolute beginners and new learners. We have received a good feedback from people using our 'Learn 35 Words to Speak' system.

If you spot errors, please let us know. If you want to suggest corrections and improvements, or even just make general comments, please send them to us at:

peter.roberts@russetpublishing.com

Of course, if you have enjoyed our book, and if it helped you to enjoy your holiday, please let us know. Many thanks.

Don't forget to learn the 35 words thoroughly *before* your holiday if you possibly can. On the other hand, perhaps it will wile away the time while you are there in a cafe in the rain, or under a sun umbrella on a hot beach, where you can order your glass of water or cup of coffee fluently in either venue.

Wherever you read it, we are sure that, when you have studied it, it will make all the difference. And remember that a language book will mean more to you and will help you to remember vocabulary if you write notes in it and add your own words and phrases!

Best wishes from Peter and Helena Roberts.

Professional Input. *The German content of this booklet has been checked, corrected, and approved by a professional translation firm using a native-speaking German, certified translator.*

CONTENTS 5

INTRODUCTION 7

Chapter 1
LEARN THE 35 WORDS 9

Chapter 2
I WANT SOMETHING 17

Chapter 3
I WANT TO FIND SOMETHING 21

Chapter 4
I WANT TO BUY SOMETHING 25

Chapter 5
I WANTED TO SPEAK GERMAN 29

INTRODUCTION

Learn 35 words. Speak German

Yes, really! If you learn the 35 words that this book contains, you will be able to speak more German than you ever thought possible in such a short time!

Try it and see. It will work! I (Peter) did learn it when we wrote this book. Now I can speak quite good 'vacation' German.

Yes, it will take some time to learn 35 words, but it will be worth it the minute you arrive in Germany and start to speak in German! We'll show you how!

This book was prepared by us to help you get around more easily. We know that within only one week, you will be able to ask for things in restaurants and in the market. You will ask directions, buy tickets, get on a train and arrive at the required destination, and have a good time.

That's why we printed this small booklet—so that anyone who wants to have a holiday in Germany, and who doesn't know any German, can 'have a go'. With confidence!

Chapter 1 of the book contains the list of 35 words that you will need to know, together with a phonetic guide to their pronunciation. You will find it easy to learn them—make sure you learn them with the correct pronunciation.
Remember, **pronunciation and emphasis are both very important**. Look at the phonetic part and practise each word <u>faster and faster</u> until it sounds like a single word.

When you have learned the list and tested yourself thoroughly, you can move on to Chapters 2, 3, and 4, which will show you how to use the 35 words so that you will be understood for most of what you will need on a German holiday. And finally, we suggest a few words that you might find useful, by starting off your list of 'dictionary' words.

Why only 35 words?

Because then you won't have to struggle with a phrase book when you want to speak! No waiter, bus conductor, or German citizen is going to hang about while you struggle in a book to find the phrase you want, is he?

We hope that you have a wonderful visit to Germany, and that upon your return our little booklet encourages you to have lessons and *really* learn how to speak the language.

Peter and Helena.

Chapter 1
Learn the 35 words.
Here's the magic list.

Unfortunately, there is no other way to learn this list but to sit down and study it for a few days. Our suggestion is that you set aside a regular time each day with someone else—preferably your proposed travel partner—and learn and test each other until you are absolutely sure that you know all of the words and can say their pronunciation correctly without thinking. Then you are ready to move on to Chapter 2.

The List

Don't forget that, in order to help you with the pronunciation, we have given a sort of amateur way of pronouncing each word, and **we have underlined the part of the word that needs speaking strongly. i.e. emphasised.** Practise until you can say each word quickly, and until you have remembered all of the words. English is in normal font; German is in italics.

For pronunciation, see pages 13 and 14, which you **should** study first, before learning the list.

1	**a**	*ein*
	pronounced:	ine (i as in English fine)
2	**also**	*auch*
	pronounced:	owch (pronounce *ch* as in loch)
3	**and**	*und*
	pronounced:	unt (*u* as in put, or foot)
4	**the bill**	*die <u>Rech</u>nung*
	pronounced:	dee <u>rech</u>-nung (*ch* as in loch)
5	**but**	*<u>a</u>ber*
	pronounced:	<u>a</u>-bur (*u* as in the English burr)
6	**cold**	*kalt*
	pronounced:	kalt
7	**do you have…?**	*<u>ha</u>ben Sie?*
	pronounced:	<u>haa</u>-ben zee?
8	**excuse me**	*ent<u>schul</u>digung*
	pronounced:	ent-<u>shul</u>-di-gung
9	**exit**	*<u>Aus</u>gang*
	pronounced:	<u>ouse</u>-gang (ouse like house)
10	**free of charge**	*<u>kos</u>tenlos*
	pronounced:	<u>kost</u>-un-lawz
11	**a glass**	*ein Glas*
	pronounced:	ine glass (i as in English fine)

12	**good**		*gut*
		pronounced:	goot
13	**good evening**		*guten Abend*
		pronounced:	goot'n ah-b'nt ('oo' as in pool)
14	**good morning**		*guten Morgen*
		pronounced:	goot'n morg'n
15	**hot** temperature		*heiss* (*würzig*) spicy
		pronounced:	high-ss (vurt-zig)
16	**how much** [is it?]		*wie viel [kostet das?]*
		pronounced:	vee feel [kost-et das?]
17	**is** [**are**]		*ist [sind]*
		pronounced:	ist [zint]
	is there a...		*gibt es ein...* (*gibt es ein Glas?*)
		pronounced:	gibt es eye-n... (is there a glass?)
18	**no**		*nein*
		pronounced:	nine
19	**of**		Not used in general speaking. Just put two nouns together, e.g. *ein Glas Bier* Or a piece of cake - *ein Stück Kuchen*
20	**one** (1)		*ein*
		pronounced:	ine
21	**or**		*oder*
		pronounced:	odour

22	**please**	_bitte_
	pronounced:	<u>bit</u>-uh
23	**small**	_klein_
	pronounced:	kline (as in fine)
24	**station**	_Bahnhof_
	pronounced:	<u>baan</u>-hoff (train station)
		Polizeistation (police station)
	pronounced:	Pol-its-eye-<u>shtats</u>-ee-on
25	**thank you**	_danke_
	pronounced:	<u>dank</u>-uh (u as in pup)
26	**that one**	_das dort_
	pronounced:	das daught (as in naught or port)
27	**the**	_der, das, die_ (different gender)
	pronounced:	dare, das, dee (m, f, neuter & plrl)
28	**this** (this one here)	_dieses hier_
	pronounced:	<u>dee</u>-suz <u>hee</u>-ur
29	**ticket**	_Fahrkarte_
	pronounced:	<u>far</u>-kart-uh (u as in pup)
30	**the toilets** (public)	_die Toiletten_
	pronounced:	dee toy-<u>let</u>-un (u as in pup)
31	**the train to**	_der Zug nach..._
	pronounced:	dare tzook naach... (_ch_ as in loch)

32 **two** (2)   zwei
         pronounced: tsvy (if too hard, say 'svy')

33 **I want** (would like)   ich *möchte*...
         pronounced: ich muucht-uh (*ch* as in loch)

    I do not want   ich *möchte* nicht...
         pronounced: ich muucht-uh nicht (*ch* as in loch)

34 **where?** [where is?]   wo   *[wo ist]*
         pronounced: vo   [vo ist]

            [where are?]   *[wo sind]*
         pronounced: [vo sint]

35 **yes**   ja
         pronounced: ya

Note that all written nouns in German start with a capital letter.

To help with your pronunciation:

The couple *'ch'* is pronounced as in the Scottish word 'loch'.

The letter *'e'* at the end of a word is pronounced as in the English utterance 'uh'. With the uh sounding like English u in *puppy*. So the German word *bitte* is pronounced bit-uh, or even like the English word bitter.

Where a letter *'s'* comes before a consonant such as *'t'* or *'p'*, then the *'s'* is pronounced as sh. So *stück* is pronounced sh-took.

Umlauts on the letter *'o'* such as in the word <u>*möchte*</u> make the letter *'o'* sound like a long version of the English 'u' as in 'purr'. So <u>*möchte*</u> sounds like muucht-uh. (ch as in loch, not chord.)

Umlauts on the letter *'u'* such as in the word *stück* make the letter *'ü'* sound like the English 'u' as in 'took' or 'put'. So *stück* sounds like sh-took. (with the *'s'* pronounced as in the English word 'shall'.)

The Germans give slightly more emphasis to the letter *'r'* than the English, but the German language doesn't emphasise *'r'* heavily as does Spanish, for example. Nonetheless an *'r'* at the end of a word is spoken gently. So that the German word *hier* is pronunced <u>hee</u>-er, with the *'r'* being sounded quietly.

English people are often confused as to how to pronounce German words that contain the letters *ie* or *ei*. The pronunciation rule is that we pronounce the couple based on the last letter of the two. So that the couple *'ie'* is pronounced *ee* and *'ei'* is pronounce as in the English word 'eye'. This settles the problem of how to pronounce the name of the famous German wine *'Riesling'*. Should we say 'Rise-ling' or should we say 'Rees-ling'? Using our rule, we look at the last letter of the pair *ie* and pronounce the pair based upon the last letter *'e'*. So it is pronounced 'Rees-ling'. OK?

Please note that German is a meticulous language that carries many detailed rules of pronunciation. We have limited our information to the words included within the book. If you learn German properly, you will need to study its pronunciation carefully, and learn from a good teacher.

- - - - - - - - oOo - - - - - - - -

So, have you really learned the magic 35 words? Or perhaps not!

If you have not, then go back to the list and keep learning until you can recall the words with no difficulty.

As we said before, learning the list is the hardest part of this job, but it won't take long if you really work at it. The morning time is the best time to learn things—when you are fresh. It's hard work in the evening when you're tired. So, find the first morning that you can—preferably before you go on holiday—and start to learn the list of 35 words. Then re-learn them the day after, and the day after and the day after. Five half hour sessions over five days will be much better than one two-and-a-half hour session.

Of course, it's even possible to learn the words while you're on holiday. At least you'll have some time to do it.

If possible, ask a friend to test you, until you are perfect.

Normally, to speak German, you will need about three years of hard effort and a private tutor. Most people don't want to put in that kind of effort or expense. For a first holiday to a different country, it's not necessary either. We know, because we've tried it.

On the other hand, it's frustrating on a holiday if you can't speak anything at all, and you feel you'd like to try to say something in German in a café, at a station, in the city, or when you want to buy something at a countryside stall or in a village shop. So, the following chapters show you how to put 35 words together to speak German! It's true!

Now that you have learned the magic 35 words, it will take you next to no time to learn how to string them together to say lots of useful things. You will be speaking German in no time at all.

OK! Now we'll show you how to put the words together to speak German!

Chapter 2
I want something.
Don't we all?

Yes we all want something—mostly all of the time. We need a drink of water—especially in the summer in Germany.

We need to ask for lots of things like drinks, food, tickets in stations, the bill in a café, and so on.

OK. Believe it or not you already know how to do this!

I want….. It's a very useful statement, but it sounds a bit brusque in English, so we exchange it for the phrase 'I would like to have". That's better! And in German, we have to use the two words *'Ich möchte'*. You want something and it says it politely.

'Ich möchte'. I want.   That's it—it's in the list of 35 words.

What do you want? Lots of things, especially a drink of tea or coffee. You already know the word for tea—we didn't have to put it on our list. It's *Tee* (pronounced tay).

Or, rather than saying that you actually want something, you can say, in a less direct way, while you consider things:

<u>Haben</u> Sie …? which simply asks, "Do you have…?
             (Pronounced <u>haa</u>-bun zee)

or, even more briefly, you can just ask '*gibt es …?*' which means 'are there…?' or 'is there…?'

Do you have tea?	*Gibt es Tee?* (Gibt es tay?)
Is there tea?	*Gibt es Tee?* (Gibt es tay?)
Is there an apple?	*Gibt es ein Apfel?* (ine Ap-fell)
Are there apples?	*Gibt es Apfel?*
Is there decaf coffee?	*Gibt es decaf Kaffee?*
	(Gibt es dee-caf ka-fay?)
Tea please.	*Tee bitte* (tay bit-uh)
Green tea	*grüner Tee* (grooner tay)

You can also specify the teabag out of the water by saying,
"Please put the teabag outside the tea pot."
"*Bitte legen Sie den Teebeutel ausserhalb der Teekanne.*"
Bit-uh lay-gen zee den tay-boy-tel owss-ur-halb dare tay-kan-uh,

That's it, and it says it all doesn't it? You can already order some tea in a cafe. And they will understand what you want. You'll get your tea the way you like it.

There is also coffee *(Kaffee)*, pronounced ka-fay.
If you want black coffee, the Germans say '*schwarzer Kaffee*'
… (pronounced shv-art-sur ka-fay)
and for white coffee, they say '*Kaffee mit Milch*'
 (pronounced Ka-fay mit Milch)   (*ch* as in loch)

I want one black coffee.
Ich möchte einen schwarzen Kaffee
with sugar   *mit Zucker* (pronounced mit zucker)
with milk   *mit Milch* (*ch* pronounced as in loch)
without caffeine   *entkoffeinierten* (ent-koff-ine-ee-ear-tun)

And to top it off and make it sound even more polite, we add the words for 'please' – *bitte* (bit-uh)

Ich möchte 'einen schwarzen Kaffee, bitte
I want one black coffee, please.

Ich möchte einen Kaffee mit Milch, bitte
I would like a white coffee, please.

Ich möchte ein Glas Wasser, bitte
I want a glass of water please. (*Wasser* pronounced 'vass-uh')

Ich möchte ein Glass Wasser mit Gas, bitte
('*mit Gas*' means 'with gas')
I want a glass of sparkling mineral water please

Ich möchte ein Glas Wasser ohne Gas, bitte
('*ohne Gas*' means 'without gas') (*Ohne* pronounced 'owner')
I want a glass of still water please.

Ich möchte zwei Limonaden (pronounced lee-mon-aa-dun), *bitte*.
I want two lemonades, please.

Ich möchte die Rechnung, bitte (dee rech-nung) (*ch* as in loch)
I want the bill please - in the restaurant or bar.

And you can also say that you don't want something.
Ich möchte nicht rotwein. (*nicht* means 'not') (*ch* as in loch)
I don't want red wine.

That's it—you are in control of the situation in the cafe. And you always added 'please' - *bitte* and 'thank you' - *danke*.

ADD YOUR OWN NOTES AND NEW WORDS HERE:

Chapter 3
To find something.
We often need to find places.

We all need to find something—mostly all of the time.

We need to know where to get a train, or a taxi, or where to buy a paper or a stamp. We need to find the right train. We need to find a garage. We need to ask for lots of things.

Most commonly, in our experience, we need to find the ladies or gents toilets.

No problem. You already know how to do this from your list of 35 words. You did say you'd learned them didn't you?

Wo ist - 'where is' and *Wo sind* 'where are'
Pronounced: vo ist and vo sint

It's pretty easy.

Wo ist das Hot<u>e</u>l?   Where is the hotel?
Wo ist ein <u>Tax</u>i?   Where is a taxi?

Or, you could try a phrase we use very often, which asks if there is a certain thing nearby. Use '*in der Nähe'* meaning 'nearby'.
Gibt es ein <u>Tax</u>i in der <u>Näh</u>e?   (pronounced 'in dare <u>nay</u>-huh')
Is there a taxi nearby?

Gibt es eine Apotheke in der Nähe?
(*eine Apotheke* pronounced 'ine-uh apo-take-uh')
Is there a pharmacy nearby?

Wo sind die Toiletten, bitte? Where are the toilets, please?
(*sind* is pronounced zint)
Öffentliche Toiletten. (Urfunt-lich-uh toy-let-un) Public toilets.
Wo ist die Toilette, bitte? Where is the toilet, please?

It's not worth learning the words for male and female because 99% of toilet doors in public places have a symbol of a man or a woman on them—standard all over the world. You'll see which door is right for you when you get there!

Men is *'Herren'* and Women is *'Frauen'*, if there is nothing pictorial on the door.

Wo ist der Bahnhof? (baan-hoff)
Where is the train station?

Wo ist die Busstation? (Bus-shtatz-ee-own) (*Bus* as English put)
Where is the bus station?

Wo ist die Bushaltestelle (Bus-hal-tuh-shtell-uh)
Where is the bus stop?

Wo ist eine Bank?
Where is a bank?

Wo ist das Hilton Hotel?
Where is the Hilton Hotel?

Of course, we can add 'please' to make it more polite.

Wo ist das Hilton Hotel, bitte?
Where is the Hilton Hotel, please?

Wo ist der Eingang?   Pronounced: ine-gang (*ine* as in nine)
Where is the entrance?

Wo ist der Ausgang?   Pronounced: ows-gang (*ows* as in house)
Where is the exit?

Anyone who speaks fluent German will tell you that the above sentences are basic. But they will work! That's the main thing. They are not grammatically perfect, but they will allow you to be understood.

In Germany, you could, of course, simply speak English, since many people understand and speak it, but that's not what you are trying to achieve, is it? You are trying to show respect to the German people, and have some enjoyment at the same time, by speaking a few words of the German language. That's why you bought this book, after all.

ADD YOUR OWN NOTES AND NEW WORDS HERE:

....
....
....
....
....
....
....
....
....
....
....
....
....
....

Chapter 4
To buy something.
Don't we all want to do that?

Yes we all want to buy something during our holidays—mostly all of the time. We need to buy presents, food, tickets, papers, postcards, et cetera.

So we could try to teach you a list of a hundred different things that you might want to buy. However, to save you the trouble most of the time, you can learn two words that will stand in for nearly everything: 'this', and 'that'.

Nonetheless, if you're smart, you'll buy a small, English/German/English pocket dictionary from your local bookshop before you visit Germany. Then you'll have a list of thousands of things that you can ask for.

Ultimately, of course, you can use your finger to point to something when you want it.

I want this! or I want that! It's easy in English—and in German

You learned the words on the list so…

Ich möchte dieses. (I would like this) (pronounced dee-suz)

Ich möchte das, bitte. (I would like that, please).

So, in a restaurant you can point to the menu and say
Ich m__ö__chte d__ie__ses, b__i__tte. (I would like this, please).

It's easy. Now you can ask for anything in the world that you can actually see at the time. I want this or I want that. Just point to it. What could be easier?

If you want to look up words, then that is also fine. For example, you might want to look up the word for a postcard, or a stamp, and then ask for them in the shop, because you might not be able to see a stamp to point to.

If you look up the word for stamp in a dictionary, you will find that it's called a '*Br__ie__fmarke*', pronounced 'B__ree__f-mark-uh'

So you walk up to the counter in the shop/post office and say:
Ich m__ö__chte __ei__ne Br__ie__fmarke nach Grossbritann__ie__n, b__i__tte. It is simple but they will understand you! "I want one stamp - to the United Kingdom". You are polite using '*b__i__tte*'.
(The word for Great Britain is pronounced *Gross-brit-__an__-ee-un*)

Before you buy something, you may wish to check how much it would cost. So you need the words '*wie viel*' - item 16 from the list of 35 words that you learned. Just use it followed by 'please' to simply say '*wie viel, b__i__tte*' - How much, please? Meaning 'how much does it cost, please?' Brief, but polite.

Or to be a bit more adventurous, you could say:
Wie viel k__o__stet das? How much is this?
(pronounced vee feel k__os__-tet das?)

Or when you have bought something, you could say the same: *Wie viel <u>kostet</u> das?* How much is that?

In Germany, some people may know English numbers, but most people will use German, so if you intend to stay in Germany for a while or go there occasionally, you may find it worthwhile learning at least the first five German numbers.

One	*eins*	(pronounced 'ines' with the '*s*' pronounced sharply as in song)
Two	*zwei*	(pronounced 'tsvy' or, optionally, svy)
Three	*drei*	(pronounced 'dry' as in English spy)
Four	*vier*	(pronounced 'feer' as in English fear)
Five	*fünf*	(pronounced 'funf' with the '*ü*' as in foot)

And now, you will be able to buy a round of drinks and become very popular. *Ich <u>möchte</u> fünf <u>Bier, bi</u>tte.* Five beers! Popular indeed!

But, of course, some people may speak English—especially if you ask. And, in any case, you can often see on the electronic till how much the thing is if you are buying it, so that's fairly easy!

If people were to reply to you in German, you wouldn't know enough to understand the number they say back to you—which would be a problem—and which is why we have not introduced words such as 'why?', 'how?', or 'what?'.

In the case of difficulty, just ask someone to please speak in English. They, or someone nearby might be able to. On the other hand, if you have a notebook and pencil, you could indicate that you wish them to write it down. That might help.

ADD YOUR OWN NOTES AND NEW WORDS HERE:

We are starting off a list of new words that you might have looked up in a small dictionary. Please continue adding some more as you go along.

police - *Polizei* (pol-<u>its</u>-eye)

then - *dann* (dan)

if - *wenn* (ven)

doctor - *<u>Dok</u>tor* (<u>dok</u>-tor)

hospital - *<u>Krank</u>enhaus* (krank-un-house)

café or coffee shop - *Cafe* (<u>ka</u>-fee)

restaurant - *Restaurant* (rest-or-awn)

waiter - *Kellner*   waitress - *Kellnerin* (Kell-n'rin)

ice - *Eis* (pronounced the same as the English ice)

we want - *Wir <u>möchten</u>.* (veer muucht-un) (*ch* as in loch)

....

....

....

Chapter 5
To speak German.
Your dream.

You wanted to speak German when you bought this book.

Well now you can. With just the 35 words we have taught you, you can speak an awful lot.

You won't believe it until you try, but you can get by for an entire holiday. And, if you have bought a small dictionary, you will learn another 35 words while you are away and you will be well on your way. You might even go to classes back home and improve more. Who knows?

Anyway, here are some of the things that you can now say that you never thought you would.

Ich möchte ein großer decaf Kaffee.   (dee-caf ka-fay)
I want one large decaffeinated coffee.
großer = grosser (pronounced grow-sur) means large or big.

Ich möchte zwei Tees   (*Tees* pronounced tays) (with s as in set)
I want two teas.

Wo ist der Bahnhof, bitte?
Where is the railway station, please?

Wo ist der Zug nach Berlin? (*Berlin* pronounced bear-lin)
Where is the train to Berlin?

Wie viel kostet das? Die Ansichtskarte?
(*Ansichtskarte* is pronounced an-six-kart-uh)
How much is this? The postcard?

Ich möchte die Rechnung, bitte.
I want the bill, please.

Ich möchte ein Kaffee und zwei Gläser Limonade (pronounce *Gläser* as glazer) (*Limonade* pronounced leem-on-ahd-uh)
I want one coffee and two glasses of lemonade, please.

Entschuldigung. Wo ist das Ritz Hotel, bitte?
Excuse me. Where is the Ritz hotel, please? (ent-shul-di-gung)

You get on a bus and ask the driver or passengers
'*Entschuldigung. Nach Berlin?*' (Excuse me. For Berlin?)
Simple. They will either nod and mutter '*ja*' or say '*nein*' and point you in the right direction. This should get you there.

Wo ist ein Taxi, bitte?
Where is a taxi, please?

Ich möchte ein Bier, bitte (Bier pronounced beer)
I want a beer, please.

Ich möchte zwei Biere, bitte. (*Biere* pronounced beer-uh)
I want two beers, please.

Red wine (*Rotwein*), pronounced w*rote*-vine, where *wein* means wine, and *rot* means red.

Or white wine: *Weißwein*, (*Weisswein* pronounced vice-vine.)

Ich möchte ein Glas Weißwein, bitte.
I want a glass of white wine, please.

Ich möchte eine Flasche Weißwein, bitte.
(*eine Flasche* pronounced ine-uh flash-uh)
I want a bottle of white wine please.

Don't you think that this is great? You have learned 35 words (plus a few more sneakily) and you are speaking German on your holiday. Well done!

And there are some lined and blank pages throughout this booklet where you can add your own new words. Soon you'll know a lot more than the 35 core words in the list. In fact, we have already offered you another 35 words in the sections on how to use the language. Just keep going!

Please remember that what you have learned here is very basic and is just a start. To speak German well, you need to read proper textbooks and go to classes with a good teacher. Or even take private lessons. We hope we have given you the incentive to do so.

But, if you don't study the language more deeply, you can always take our booklet with you when you go to Germany again!

With best wishes,

Peter and Helena.

www.ingramcontent.com/pod-product-compliance
Lightning Source LLC
Chambersburg PA
CBHW071804040426
42446CB00012B/2710